How to Play Funny Fill-In!

Love to create amazing stories? Good, because this one stars YOU. Get ready to laugh with all your friends—you can play with as many people as you want! Make sure to keep this book on your shelf. You'll want to read it again and again!

Are You Ready to Laugh?

- One person picks a story—you can start at the beginning, the middle, or the end of the book.

- Ask a friend to call out a word that the space asks for—noun, verb, or something else—and write it in the blank space. If there's more than one person, ask the next person to say a word. Extra points for creativity!

- When all the spaces are filled in, you have your very own Funny Fill-In. Read it out loud for a laugh.

- Want to play by yourself? Just fold over the page and use the cardboard insert at the back as a writing pad. Fill in the blank parts of speech list, and copy your answers into the story.

Fun Fact! Make sure you check out the amazing **Fun Facts** that appear on every page!

Parts of Speech

To play the game, you'll need to know how to form sentences. This list of the parts of speech and the examples will help you get started:

Noun: The name of a person, place, thing, or idea
Examples: tree, mouth, creature
*The **ocean** is full of colorful **fish**.*

Adjective: A word that describes a noun or pronoun
Examples: green, lazy, friendly
*My **silly** dog won't stop laughing!*

Verb: An action word. In the present tense, a verb usually ends in –s or –ing. If the space asks for past tense, changing the vowel or adding a –d or –ed to the end usually will set the sentence in the past.
Examples: swim, hide, play (present tense);
biked, rode, jumped (past tense)
*The giraffe **skips** across the savanna.*
*The flower **opened** after the rain.*

Adverb: A word that describes a verb and usually ends in –ly
Examples: quickly, lazily, soundlessly
*Kelley **greedily** ate all the carrots.*

Plural: More than one
Examples: mice, telephones, wrenches
*Why are all the **doors** closing?*

Silly Word or Exclamation: A funny sound, a made-up word, a word you think is totally weird, or a noise someone or something might make
Examples: Ouch! No way! Foozleduzzle! Yikes!
*"**Darn!**" shouted Jim. "These cupcakes are sour!"*

Specific Words: There are many more ways to make your story hilarious. When asked for something like a number, animal, or body part, write in something you think is especially funny.

- adjective
  - animal
- verb ending in –ing
  - verb
- friend's name
  - relative's name
- number
  - adjective
- silly word
  - verb
- direction
  - one of the Wonders of the World
- body part
  - your name
- celebrity's name
  - kind of lunch meat
- favorite movie
  - favorite snack

MORE THAN 60,000 PEOPLE ARE FLYING OVER THE UNITED STATES IN AIRPLANES RIGHT NOW.

The Adventure Begins

No way! I won the _____ _____ contest! I can't believe it. For my prize, I'll be _____
                     adjective   animal   verb ending in –ing

around the world to _____ all the coolest animals. Of course, I'm bringing _____ .
                         verb   friend's name

Unfortunately, there's so much luggage, it takes _____ and _____ neighbors to jam it
                                                    relative's name   number

all into the car. Finally on the road, everything is going as planned. Until the GPS goes _____ and
                                                                                              adjective

starts saying things like, "_____ _____ _____ ." Following the bewildering
                              silly word   verb   direction

commands, we pass _____ ! But, finally, the airport comes into view. Just as I
                     one of the Wonders of the World

squeeze my _____ into the airplane seat, the loudspeaker crackles and I hear, "_____ ,
               body part   your name

raise your hand." Turns out, _____ has decided (s)he only rides on airplanes the color of
                               celebrity's name

_____ . We get moved to his/her first class seats! Seat back, feet up, _____
kind of lunch meat   favorite movie

on the screen, munching on _____ —I could get used to this!
                              favorite snack

- verb ending in –ing
  - friend's name
- favorite song
  - animal
- noun
  - famous sports player
- verb
  - body part
- loud noise
  - color
- adjective
  - number
- noun
  - something smelly
- item of clothing, plural
  - adjective
- adjective
  - verb ending in –ing
- singer's name

Fun Fact! WHEN A BROWN BEAR **STANDS** ON ITS **HIND LEGS,** IT'S NOT ALWAYS TRYING TO BE **THREATENING.** IT'S OFTEN JUST GETTING **A BETTER LOOK AT ITS SURROUNDINGS.**

Over-BEAR-ing Family Photo

Our first stop, backpacking in Alaska! With my camera _____ around my neck, _____
                                        verb ending in –ing   friend's name

is singing _____ as we walk down the trail. Too bad that his/her singing sounds more like a
             favorite song

_____ . I decide to check out a cool _____ I see in the distance. But, as I walk farther,
animal   noun

a bear bigger than _____ _____ in front of me. I am so scared, I feel as if my
                  famous sports player   verb

_____ is jelly! Suddenly, I hear a(n) _____ , and _____ fur and
body part   loud noise   color

_____ teeth surround me. _____ bears are so close I can feel their
adjective   number

_____ and smell their _____ breath! Then the bears put on wacky
noun   something smelly

_____ and _____ sunglasses. They start posing with _____ smiles as
item of clothing, plural   adjective   adjective

if they're on vacation! Finally, I realize they are _____ and want photos. Just then, my
                                        verb ending in –ing

friend arrives, still singing. The bears join in. Mother Bear sounds just like _____ !
                                                       singer's name

- adjective
  - silly word
- size
  - electronic gadget
- body part
  - relative's name
- item of clothing
  - adverb ending in –ly
- cartoon show
  - verb
- verb
  - food
- noun
  - noun
- verb ending in –ing
  - another item of clothing
- noun
  - noun

Fun Fact! BLACK-TAILED PRAIRIE DOGS **WARN EACH OTHER** AT THE **FIRST SIGN** OF **PREDATORS,** SUCH AS A HUNGRY HAWK OR BLACK-FOOTED FERRET.

Prairie Dog Pranksters

The North American grasslands are _____ . Thanks to prankster prairie dogs, I now have a new video.
                                  adjective

Just not exactly what I'd hoped. As we crept into _____ -ville, a(n) _____ prairie dog popped out
                                                   silly word   size

of its burrow and snatched my _____ . When I dove into the praire dog's tunnel, my
                               electronic gadget

_____ got wedged in the opening. _____ grabbed my feet but instead accidentally
 body part   relative's name

pulled off my _____ . The prairie dog took a picture, then _____ disappeared
               item of clothing   adverb ending in –ly

underground. What happened next was like a _____ chase. I'd _____ . The animal
                                            cartoon show   verb

would _____ . Each time, its friend snapped pictures. They grabbed my _____ , my
        verb   food

_____ , and my favorite _____ ! Finally, a prairie dog stood on top of me, _____
 noun   noun   verb ending in –ing

my cellphone, recording video, and wearing my _____ , my _____ , and even my
                                               another item of clothing   noun

_____ . Suddenly, it started typing on my phone. It hit "Send." Wouldn't you know, the video went viral!
 noun

- small number
  - pop star
- loud noise
  - noun
- friend's name
  - noun
- piece of furniture
  - verb ending in –ing
- adjective
  - body part
- liquid
  - verb ending in –ing
- verb
  - adjective
- something gross
  - animal, plural
- verb
  - animal

Fun Fact! A DAIRY COW **PRODUCES** ABOUT **100,000** **GLASSES OF MILK** **IN ITS LIFETIME.**

Farm Frenzy

At _____ a.m., we pile into the car for a canoe trip. We are singing along to _____
_{small number} ... _{pop star}

when we hear a(n) _____. Our car has a flat _____! Soon, a pickup truck pulls
_{loud noise} ... _{noun}

over. "I'm Farmer _____. Can I offer y'all a ride?" the driver asks. That's how we spent
_{friend's name}

the day on a _____ farm. I sit on a(n) _____ next to the farmer to learn to
_{noun} ... _{piece of furniture}

milk a cow. But the cow starts _____ my hair. So instead, I try to run the _____
_{verb ending in –ing} ... _{adjective}

milk machine. As I pull a lever, my _____ disconnects a tube, and _____
_{body part} ... _{liquid}

starts _____ everywhere. I _____ from the machine, right into
_{verb ending in –ing} ... _{verb}

a(n) _____ pile of _____. A bunch of _____
_{adjective} ... _{something gross} ... _{animal, plural}

run to lap up the spill, so I _____ toward the door. On the way,
_{verb}

I slip and fall into the _____ pen. Who knew a farm was this wild?
_{animal}

11

- something scary
- friend's name
- noun
- relative's name
- adverb ending in –ly
- sound
- verb
- something gross
- same friend
- something silly
- verb
- sports star
- adverb ending in –ly
- feeling
- number
- toy
- adjective

Fun Fact! ONE WOLF CAN EAT **20 POUNDS** (9 KG) OF FOOD AT A TIME—THAT'S ABOUT **80 HAMBURGERS!**

Wolf Games

Towering over us, the shaggy wolf casts a shadow creepier than _____ . _____
                                                                    something scary   *friend's name*

immediately climbs up a(n) _____ , and I manage to grab on to a tree limb. While I dangle like
                                noun

_____ 's ugly earrings, the wolf snaps at my feet. Panicking, I _____
    relative's name   *adverb ending in –ly*

fling my shoe. The creature catches it with a loud _____ and _____ it. Dropping to
                                                        sound   *verb*

the ground, I run, but choke on the overpowering smell of _____ odor from the shoe.
                                                              something gross

_____ yells, "_____ ," and _____ his/her shoe.
    same friend   *something silly*   *verb*

The wolf catches it in midair like _____ ! _____ carrying
                                        sports star   *adverb ending in –ly*

the shoe, the wolf is as _____ as a _____ -year-old with a new _____ .
                              feeling   *number*   *toy*

A game of fetch is what this pooch wants! Our shoes end up a bit _____ , but we have fun
                                                                      adjective

playing with our new friend.

adjective

    noun, plural

adjective

    verb

noun

    body part

animal

    number

ice-cream flavor

    verb

friend's name

    something gross

mythical creature

    liquid

noun

    adverb ending in –ly

verb

    same friend

Fun Fact! AN ALLIGATOR **GROWS** ABOUT **3,000** TEETH IN A **LIFETIME.**

Dangerous Dentistry

My next adventure is in the swampy Florida Everglades! Our boat skims across the _____ water.
adjective

Mosquitoes as big as _____ zoom by our heads. Suddenly, a(n) _____ alligator pops
noun, plural _adjective_

out of the water! I think he is going to _____ me. Instead, he sobs like a(n) _____ and
verb _noun_

points to his mouth with his _____. Fortunately, I've seen every episode of _____
body part _animal_

Whisperer on channel _____, so I know his tooth hurts. But when I get close with my _____-
number _ice-cream flavor_

flavored dental floss, he _____ his mouth shut. Just then, _____ slips
verb _friend's name_

on _____, shrieks like a _____, then falls into some _____.
something gross _mythical creature_ _liquid_

The alligator laughs so hard his mouth opens wider than a(n) _____. Here's my chance!
noun

I _____ lasso the tooth. It pops right out. Just then, the alligator's mom _____
adverb ending in –ly _verb_

through the water toward _____. That's how I discover my friend is faster than a boat!
same friend

- your weight
  - large number
- friend's name
  - adjective
- color
  - color
- adjective
  - feeling
- sound ending in –ing
  - adverb ending in –ly
- number
  - direction
- adjective
  - favorite frozen dessert
- verb
  - famous artist

Fun Fact! POLAR BEARS HAVE **TRANSPARENT HAIR** WITH A HOLLOW CORE THAT **REFLECTS SUNLIGHT,** MAKING THEM APPEAR TO BE WHITE; THEIR SKIN IS **ACTUALLY BLACK!**

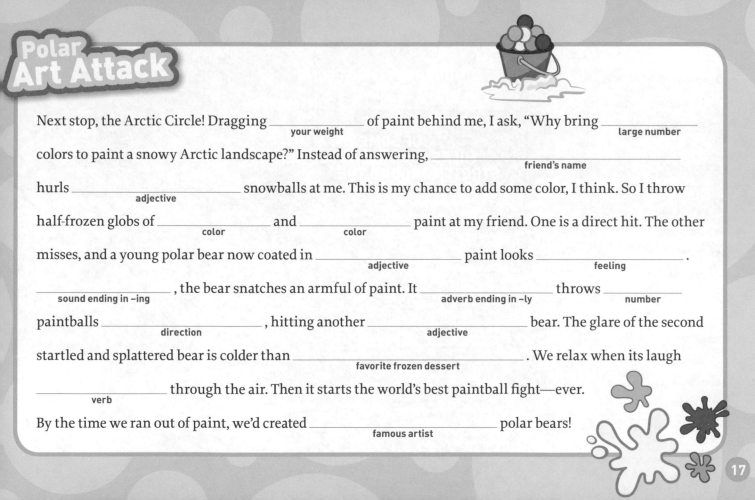

Polar Art Attack

Next stop, the Arctic Circle! Dragging _____ of paint behind me, I ask, "Why bring _____
your weight   *large number*

colors to paint a snowy Arctic landscape?" Instead of answering, _____
friend's name

hurls _____ snowballs at me. This is my chance to add some color, I think. So I throw
adjective

half-frozen globs of _____ and _____ paint at my friend. One is a direct hit. The other
color   *color*

misses, and a young polar bear now coated in _____ paint looks _____ .
adjective   *feeling*

_____ , the bear snatches an armful of paint. It _____ throws _____
sound ending in –ing   *adverb ending in –ly*   *number*

paintballs _____ , hitting another _____ bear. The glare of the second
direction   *adjective*

startled and splattered bear is colder than _____ . We relax when its laugh
favorite frozen dessert

_____ through the air. Then it starts the world's best paintball fight—ever.
verb

By the time we ran out of paint, we'd created _____ polar bears!
famous artist

- animal sound
  - friend's name
- adjective ending in –est
  - noun
- something soft
  - mythical creature, plural
- baby animal, plural
  - kind of candy
- pet's name
  - silly word
- verb
  - verb
- something scary
  - animal, plural
- something sharp
  - adjective
- verb
  - noun

EUROPE IS THE SECOND **SMALLEST** CONTINENT—BUT ITS COASTLINE OF SOME **24,000** MILES (38,000 KM) WOULD NEARLY STRETCH AROUND THE **EARTH.**

Cute Overload

We're trekking across the European countryside, and as we round the hedge, a soft _____ ,

animal sound

fills the air. _____ and I creep toward the sweet sound. Hanging out along a river are the world's

friend's name

_____ creatures. Their _____ and soft _____ invite us

adjective ending in –est   *noun*   *something soft*

closer. Some wrestle like _____ . Others cuddle like _____ .

mythical creature, plural   *baby animal, plural*

And, they smell like _____ . One reminds me of _____ . I can't help it,

kind of candy   *pet's name*

I yell, "_____ !" All eyes _____ at us. That's when those sweet

silly word   *verb*

fuzzy faces _____ into _____ ! Now, a herd of ferocious

verb   *something scary*

stuffed _____ with _____ teeth and _____

animal, plural   *something sharp*   *adjective*

claws are chasing us! We sprint and see the edge of a cliff—we _____ , splashing

verb

into the water below. Never judge a _____ by its cute looks!

noun

type of transportation

relative's name

loud noise

sharp object

friend's name

three letters

number

color

verb

adjective ending in –est

item of clothing, plural

electronic gadget, plural

amount of time

number

adverb ending in –ly

verb

same three letters

noun, plural

Fun Fact!

ADULT MALE
MANDRILL MONKEYS
HAVE RED-AND-BLUE
NOSES. THE COLOR
BECOMES BRIGHTER WHEN
THEY ARE EXCITED
OR UPSET.

Monkey Mechanics

It's our first day in Africa, and our safari _____ , which is older than _____ ,
                                            type of transportation   *relative's name*

rattles down the jungle road. Suddenly, all four tires pop with a(n) "_____ !" when we cross
                                                                     loud noise

_____ Point. _____ radios _____ -Primate tire service, which
sharp object   *friend's name*   *three letters*

advertises its mechanics are "terribly fast." Within seconds, I hear something. _____ _____
                                                                               number   *color*

monkeys _____ from the trees. The _____ yanks us out of the vehicle.
        verb   *adjective ending in −est*

_____ and _____ fly through the air. Within
item of clothing, plural   *electronic gadget, plural*

_____ , a monkey hands me a $ _____ bill for the "terribly fast" service.
amount of time   *number*

The monkeys _____ _____ up the trees. True to its advertising,
            adverb ending in −ly *verb*

_____ -Primate service is definitely fast. Unfortunately, it's really terrible, too.
same three letters

The monkeys replaced the flat tires with _____ !
                                          noun, plural

- adjective
  - celebrity's name
- verb ending in –ing
  - verb
- number
  - something silly
- adverb ending in –ly
  - verb
- insect, plural
  - food
- noun
  - kind of candy
- adjective
  - something gross
- body part, plural

Fun Fact! THE **LARGEST** LAND ANIMALS ON EARTH, AFRICAN ELEPHANTS USE THEIR **TRUNKS TO SPRAY WATER** TO KEEP COOL.

Elephant Edibles

Now that we've properly fixed our tires, I brought a ridiculously _____ bag of peanuts for our
                                                                    adjective

drive over to the _____ Preserve to care for African elephants. But while everyone else
                        celebrity's name

is _____ , I decide to sneak a snack. I _____ into my first peanut when
        verb ending in –ing   *verb*

_____ hungry elephants step out of the brush in front of the car. I shout, "_____"
    number   *something silly*

and _____ drop the sack of snacks. Peanuts tumble everywhere. Elephant trunks
            adverb ending in –ly

_____ all over me like _____ . But now the peanuts are gone, and the
        verb   *insect, plural*

elephants are still hungry! Looking for more, the herd flips the jeep and shakes it like a box of _____
                                                                                                        food

with a _____ inside. As I dangle from my seatbelt, _____ slip from my shirt
            noun   *kind of candy*

pocket, to the elephants' delight. I now know they have _____ tongues and breath like
                                                                adjective

_____ . But they put me down safely and smack their _____ , leaving me starving!
    something gross   *body part, plural*

- liquid
  - type of sandwich
- cool word
  - movie star
- body part
  - adjective
- adjective
  - something gross
- fictional villain
  - verb
- noun
  - food
- silly word
  - verb ending in –ing
- verb ending in –ing
  - animal
- verb
  - type of insect

Fun Fact! AN **OSTRICH** CAN RUN AS FAST AS A **RACEHORSE.**

Ostrich Race

It's another hot African day, and I'm drinking lots of _____ . Nearby, I see a group of ostriches, and
                                                        liquid

I turn to see one munching on my _____ . "Wanna race?" he says. "_____ !"
                                              type of sandwich   cool word

I say. My ostrich is _____ cool and so tall I only come up to his _____ .
                                movie star   body part

I'm tied to him with a _____ rope. The team next to us is _____ . There's a kid
                                adjective   adjective

who has _____ hair and a _____ -mean face. We _____
                something gross   fictional villain   verb

down the track, when suddenly the tough kid sticks out a _____ , causing us to stumble into a
                                                                          noun

_____ stand. The crowd chants, "_____ faces lose races!" _____ ,
            food   silly word   verb ending in –ing

_____ , and sidestepping the mess, we cross the finish line, winning the race, and
      verb ending in –ing

whiz to the next contest. We win the _____ dance contest, too! But I had better _____
                                                    animal   verb

the fine print for the _____ race I signed up for next!
                            type of insect

type of amphibian

verb

noun

color

color

relative's name

adjective

number

body part

number

item of clothing

size

liquid

friend's name

vegetable, plural

cooking utensil, plural

your hometown

friend's name

Fun Fact!

SOME PARROTS **DANCE** WHEN THEY HEAR **POP MUSIC.**

Dropping In for Dinner

I've always wanted to see the South American rain forest! As I head to the _____ preserve,
(type of amphibian)

I see there's an option to zip line there. I _____ faster than a _____ . Just then, a _____
(verb)   (noun)   (color)

and _____ parrot lands on me and starts babbling faster than _____ about a feast.
(color)   (relative's name)

All of a sudden, I notice other animals trying to hear what's on the _____ menu. There are
(adjective)

_____ animals dangling from my _____ and _____ more latch
(number)   (body part)   (number)

on to my _____ . With so much weight, the zip line snaps! I drop into a _____ stewpot
(item of clothing)   (size)

filled with _____ that smells like _____ 's feet! A crowd gathers. Some hold
(liquid)   (friend's name)

_____ and sharp _____ . Someone says, "Ah, here is the exotic food from
(vegetable, plural)   (cooking utensil, plural)

_____ ." The crowd cheers. "Come, eat!" Uh-oh. Am I the exotic food? Just then, _____
(your hometown)   (friend's name)

walks up with the parrot. It says, "Come! Eat! My new friend, we set a special place for you!"

mythical creature

body part

adjective

big city

silly word

cartoon character

number

larger number

color

food

verb

noun

internal organ, plural

something gross

adverb ending in –ly

verb

friend's name

your name

Fun Fact!

RAIN FORESTS ARE MOST "ALIVE" AT NIGHT—
80 PERCENT OF ALL THE ANIMAL ACTIVITY
TAKES PLACE IN THE DARK.

The Coolest Species No One Ever Saw

Move over, _____ , you have competition! My hike through the remote South American
                    mythical creature

jungle has led me face-to-_____ with a brand-new species. Only, I'm sure no one will believe me.
                              body part

It's the most _____ creature I've ever seen. Its skin sparkles like _____ at night.
                 adjective   *big city*

"_____ , is my name," it says in a _____ -like voice. _____ of its
     silly word   *cartoon character*   *number*

_____ arms glow _____ . Its legs remind me of a(n) _____ . All of its eyes
 larger number   *color*   *food*

focus on me. Suddenly, it _____ through the air, whirling like a(n) _____ ,
                          verb   *noun*

and lands next to me. I could get over the eyes, arms, and visible _____ , but it smells
                                                                   internal organ, plural

like _____ . "Want to know why I'm the coolest animal ever?" it _____
      something gross   *adverb ending in –ly*

purrs. Before I can answer, my friends _____ through the trees, and it vanishes. No one believes
                                        verb

me, and _____ starts calling it the _____ -made-it-uppa monster!
          friend's name   *your name*

- noun
  - friend's name
- celebrity name, possessive
  - fruit
- adverb ending in –ly
  - transportation, plural
- verb
  - noun
- adjective
  - something in nature, plural
- verb
  - body part
- royal title
  - sound, plural
- adjective
  - something you bring to the beach
- favorite flavor
  - adverb ending in –ly

Fun Fact! **ANTS** CAN LIFT AND CARRY MORE THAN **100 TIMES** THEIR OWN WEIGHT.

Temperatures are rising faster than a(n) _____ . _____ and I can't wait to get to
                                          noun   friend's name

_____ Paradise Beach, to relax and enjoy tropical _____ smoothies.
celebrity name, possessive   fruit

_____ pedaling through the jungle on _____ , we stop at an "Ant Crossing"
adverb ending in –ly   transportation, plural

sign. We _____ a line of ants carrying so much fruit it looks like a(n) _____ . Missing
          verb   noun

_____ beach time, I create a ramp from _____ . We _____
adjective   something in nature, plural   verb

over the ants and keep going. Then I see spots! A jaguar with an injured _____ blocks the path.
                                                                          body part

Fortunately, I'm _____ of the Wildcat First Aid Club, and I heal the injured animal.
                  royal title

When we're finally greeted by the beach's _____ , I need a(n) _____ drink.
                                            sound, plural   adjective

Just as I plop into my _____ , the ants march up with a _____
                        something you bring to the beach   favorite flavor

smoothie, and my new spotted friend _____ serves it. Now that's paradise!
                                      adverb ending in –ly

sports player

sport

adjective

size

verb

adjective

adjective

noun

verb

liquid

gymnastics move

flying animal

relative's name

body part

adverb ending in –ly

color

same liquid

cool word

Fun Fact! SOME **WILD DOLPHINS PLAY CATCH** WITH **COCONUTS.**

DUDE, Dolphin Surfing

I always knew I could surf like _____ , who plays _____ ! Showing off
                                    sports player   *sport*

my _____ moves, I didn't see the _____ dolphin until I _____ him.
      adjective   *size*   *verb*

"Dude," he said. "You've got some _____ moves, but I'm better!" Dolphins may rule the
                                    adjective

surf, but I am _____ . Catching the perfect _____ , I _____ through
                 adjective   *noun*   *verb*

the _____ like a pro. Next to me, the dolphin does a spectacular _____ .
      liquid   *gymnastics move*

Launching too high, I hit a _____ . Screeching like _____ , it grabs
                             flying animal   *relative's name*

on to me, covering my _____ . I nearly fall, but the animal flies away. I'm surfing faster than
                        body part

ever, but I _____ realize I'm not controlling my _____ board. That's
              adverb ending in –ly   *color*

because I'm surfing on the dolphin! Ripping through the _____ waves, we both rule the surf.
                                                          same liquid

This is _____ !
          cool word

33

liquid

noun

musical instrument

favorite song

adjective

color

noun

pop star

number

adjective

noun

friend's name

another musical instrument

animal

type of pattern

verb

sea creature

adjective ending in –est

CORAL REEFS ARE CONSIDERED THE RAIN FORESTS OF THE SEA, BECAUSE THEY PROVIDE FOOD AND SHELTER FOR UP TO 25 PERCENT OF ALL MARINE LIFE.

Rocking the Reef

The hum of the ocean takes on new meaning as I snorkel in _____ (liquid) through an Indonesian coral reef. Admiring coral more colorful than a(n) _____ (noun), I swim around the nearest rock and hear a(n) _____ (musical instrument) -fish start playing _____ (favorite song). Then I see a seahorse strumming sea grass like a(n) _____ (adjective) guitar and a(n) _____ (color) fish belting out a(n) _____ (noun) better than _____ (pop star). The concert grows when _____ (number) tube worms pop up as background singers. This band is just getting started! Suddenly, an octopus appears in front of me and stretches across the coral to make a(n) _____ (adjective) drum so I can add a(n) _____ (noun). _____ (friend's name) plays a snorkel like a(n) _____ (another musical instrument), and a(n) _____ (animal) picks up the song's melody. A fiddler crab and electric eel rock the sea while _____ (type of pattern) fish _____ (verb). I'm almost blown back when a(n) _____ (sea creature) hits the _____ (adjective ending in -est) final note! Download the ocean band's album . . . if you have "Sea"-Tunes!

number

    adjective

friend's name

    noun

liquid

    adjective

adjective ending in –er

    verb

something pointy

    same friend

something soft

    noun

verb ending in –ed

    something in nature

body part

    noise

noun

    adjective

Fun Fact! TIGERS CAN EAT **40 POUNDS** (18 KILOGRAMS) IN A SINGLE SITTING. AFTER A BIG MEAL, THEY CAN GO UP TO **ONE WEEK** WITHOUT EATING.

We're in India, and after our _____ -mile _____ hike, _____ and I are hotter than
                                  number   adjective   friend's name

_____ . We get to the end and see a(n) _____ fountain guarded by—a tiger! "To quench your
   noun   liquid

thirst, you must answer first," announces the _____ tiger. "What gets _____ as it
                                                  adjective   adjective ending in -er

_____ ?" the big cat asks through _____ teeth. _____
   verb   something pointy   same friend

croaks, "A _____ !" The tiger nods, and immediately asks, "What runs all the _____
            something soft   noun

and never gets _____ ?" I squeak, "A _____ !" "Last question,"
                verb ending in -ed   something in nature

he declares. "Where does water leave its car?" I strain my parched brain. Nothing. Finally, I stand on my

_____ , and the answers trickles out. "A water park!" A(n) _____ blares and
  body part   noise

the _____ shakes. The fountain drops away, exposing a(n) _____ water park!
     noun   adjective

Sliding, splashing, and playing the rest of the day, I know I have never been so wet!

- silly word beginning with "Y"
- number
- relative's name
- adjective
- kind of music
- noun, plural
- animal
- direction
- noun
- noun
- internal organ, plural
- noun
- verb
- adverb ending in –ly
- adjective
- noun
- noun
- feeling

WILD YAKS
LIVE AT VERY HIGH ELEVATIONS—
UP TO 17,700 FEET
(5,395 M)!

HA!

HA!

HA!

Yucking It Up With a Yak

Crossing the Himalaya Mountains is taking forever. So are the endless jokes from _____
silly word beginning with "Y"

the yak. His jokes were fun, the first _____ miles. Too bad he is about as funny as _____ .
number   *relative's name*

Plus, my funny bone froze hours ago. His impersonations include a(n) _____ pigeon, a tiger singing
adjective

_____ , sticking _____ on his head, and his wacky Aunt _____ . As we climb
kind of music   *noun, plural*   *animal*

_____ the yak asks, "Hey, did you hear the one about...?" We yell "No more _____ !" so loud,
direction   *noun*

we almost cause a(n) _____ . "What's with the jokes?" I ask. He says, "Laughter keeps you warm."
noun

By now, even my _____ are shivering, so I grab my _____ and
internal organ, plural   *noun*

_____ _____ . Chuckles erupt from my _____ frozen friend.
verb   *adverb ending in -ly*   *adjective*

Then his/her _____ sparks and catches on fire. I laugh so hard my _____ bursts into
noun   *noun*

flames. Laughing the rest of the way, we are _____ and warm, though a bit charred!
feeling

39

- adjective ending in –est
- liquid
- verb
- number
- verb ending in –ing
- something cold
- body part
- noun
- verb ending in –ing
- number
- verb
- noun
- friend's name
- sound
- mythical creature
- favorite song
- adjective
- celebrity's name

Fun Fact! SOME PENGUINS SLIDE ON THEIR **BELLIES,** USING THEIR FEET TO PUSH THEM FORWARD.

Walking along the Antarctic coast, I look for the _____ place to photograph.
_{adjective ending in -est}

But I get too close to the _____ ! Ice starts to _____ , and before I know it—I'm adrift
_{liquid} _{verb}

on an iceberg! I turn to see black-and-white feathers. _____ pesky penguins gather on one end of the
_{number}

iceberg and start _____ like it's a trampoline! Then, the _____ sloshes
_{verb ending in -ing} _{something cold}

over my _____ because our iceberg is tipping. *Splat!* A hefty penguin plops down and
_{body part}

launches me so high into the air I think I see my _____ ! But I drop, _____
_{noun} _{verb ending in -ing}

on top of a(n) _____ -story-tall iceberg. I _____ down it faster than a(n) _____
_{number} _{verb} _{noun}

and hear _____ _____ like a(n) _____ . Penguins jump
_{friend's name} _{sound} _{mythical creature}

from iceberg to iceberg. I hear _____ and realize it's a flash mob—penguin style! The birds
_{favorite song}

fling me back into the air, and I show off my _____ moves like _____ !
_{adjective} _{celebrity's name}

adjective

   noun

verb

   same verb

number

   type of container

something gross

   verb ending in –ing

animal, plural

   noun, plural

number

   noun

adjective

   friend's name

relative's name

   adjective

number

   same type of container

Fun Fact!

KANGAROOS
CAN'T HOP
BACKWARD.

Jumping Joeys

There are some _____ animals in Australia, found nowhere else on Earth. Walking to our
(adjective)

kangaroo observation tour, I remember I left my souvenir _____ at the gift shop. I _____
(noun) _(verb)_

to catch the group, but I forget the guide's warning, "Never ever _____ near kangaroos!"
(same verb)

_____ kangaroos spring into view. One puts me into her _____, which smells like the
(number) _(type of container)_

inside of an old _____. She takes off _____ over snapping _____,
(something gross) _(verb ending in -ing)_ _(animal, plural)_

bounding through _____, and vaulting _____ feet across a(n) _____
(noun, plural) _(number)_ _(noun)_

—with me still inside! I peek out and see two other _____-eyed "joeys" with their kangaroo
(adjective)

moms. It's _____ and _____. Finally, the mama kangaroos stop in front of
(friend's name) _(relative's name)_

the _____ tour guide. They toss us to the ground and hop away. What a ride! I think I'll
(adjective)

use the _____ cents I found in my kangaroo's _____ to buy everyone a snack.
(number) _(same type of container)_

adverb ending in –ly

plant

number

adverb ending in –ly

verb

verb

noun

famous explorer

country

relative's name

silly word

noun

friend's name

animal

verb

electronic equipment

verb ending in –ing

verb

Fun Fact! **KOALAS** STAY AWAKE FOR ONLY **FOUR HOURS** A DAY.

Snoozing Through the Outback

Hurrying to the airport, we race through the Australian Outback. But we are so _____ lost.
(adverb ending in -ly)

I think we've passed the same _____ _____ times. Finally, in a panic, we stop to ask the
(plant) (number)

only living thing around, a napping koala. Jostling him awake, I beg for directions. It _____
(adverb ending in -ly)

_____ me a compass and a map. But the compass needle _____ like a(n) _____
(verb) (verb) (noun)

and the map was printed before _____ discovered _____. The koala snores
(famous explorer) (country)

louder than _____. I shake it, yelling, "_____!" until the bleary-eyed beast
(relative's name) (silly word)

hands me a chart. Unfortunately, it was a(n) _____ chart. Frustrated, _____ whacks it
(noun) (friend's name)

with a stuffed _____. Finally, the exasperated koala _____ into his pocket and
(animal) (verb)

pulls out a brand-new _____, and instantly falls asleep again. _____
(electronic equipment) (verb ending in -ing)

we make the flight—just barely. I am so tired from our adventure, I _____ just like the koala!
(verb)

45

pet's name

relative

something gross

first name starting with "L"

electronic device

verb

your street name

adjective

verb ending in –ing

color

yard tool

friend's last name

feeling

something slimy

animal

noun, plural

body part

verb

What a trip! I miss being on the road, but am glad to have my _____ ! Even _____ 's
                                                                    pet's name   *relative*

home cooking tasted better than the _____ stew we tried. I brought home a little
                                        something gross

surprise, _____ the lemur. Before I can introduce my new friend to anyone, the lemur
           first name starting with "L"

whips out a(n) _____ , then _____ it out the window. Bounding down
                electronic device   *verb*

_____ , it snaps a shot of my _____ neighbor _____ . She turns
your street name   *adjective*   *verb ending in -ing*

bright _____ and throws a(n) _____ at us. Mrs. _____ isn't _____
        color   *yard tool*   *friend's last name*   *feeling*

when the lemur accidentally knocks a bucket of _____ on her while trying to get an action
                                                 something slimy

photo. That makes the neighborhood _____ laugh so hard _____ shoot out
                                      animal   *noun, plural*

its _____ . My lemur friend _____ a photo of that, too.
     body part   *verb*

I haven't even unpacked yet, and my next adventure has already started!

Credits

Cover, Frans Lanting/National Geographic Stock; 4, karamysh/Shutterstock; 6, Michel Zoghzoghi/National Geographic Stock; 8, Eller/Shutterstock; 10, Iakov Kalinin/Shutterstock; 12, Daveallenphoto/Dreamstime; 14, Ntnstwin/Dreamstime; 16, Lanaufoto/Dreamstime; 18, VLADJ55/Shutterstock; 20, Lifeontheside/Dreamstime; 22, Duncan Noakes/Dreamstime (Background), Duncan Noakes/Dreamstime (LE); 24, Zuzana Randlova/Dreamstime; 26, Doron Rosendorff/Dreamstime; 28, Herrbullermann/Dreamstime; 30, Nolte Lourens/Dreamstime; 32, Paul Topp/Dreamstime; 34, Vilainecrevette/Dreamstime; 36, Waj/Shutterstock; 38, Bbbar/Dreamstime; 40, Maxily/Dreamstime; 42, idiz/Shutterstock; 44, Joe Hubbard/Dreamstime; 46, art&design/Shutterstock.

Published by the National Geographic Society

John M. Fahey, *Chairman of the Board and Chief Executive Officer*
Declan Moore, *Executive Vice President; President, Publishing and Travel*
Melina Gerosa Bellows, *Executive Vice President; Chief Creative Officer, Books, Kids, and Family*

Prepared by the Book Division

Hector Sierra, *Senior Vice President and General Manager*
Nancy Laties Feresten, *Senior Vice President, Kids Publishing and Media*
Jay Sumner, *Director of Photography, Children's Publishing*
Jennifer Emmett, *Vice President, Editorial Director, Children's Books*
Eva Absher-Schantz, *Design Director, Kids Publishing and Media*
R. Gary Colbert, *Production Director*
Jennifer A. Thornton, *Director of Managing Editorial*

Staff for This Book

Kate Olesin, *Project Editor*
James Hiscott, Jr., *Art Director*
Kelley Miller, *Senior Photo Editor*
Ruth Ann Thompson, *Designer*
Ariane Szu-Tu, *Editorial Assistant*
Callie Broaddus, *Design Production Assistant*
Hillary Moloney, *Illustrations Assistant*
Ruth Musgrave, *Writer*
Jason Tharp, *Illustrator*
Grace Hill and Michael O'Connor, *Associate Managing Editors*
Joan Gossett, *Production Editor*
Lewis R. Bassford, *Production Manager*
Susan Borke, *Legal and Business Affairs*
Kayla Klaben, *Intern*
Angela Modany, *Intern*

Manufacturing and Quality Management

Phillip L. Schlosser, *Senior Vice President*
Chris Brown, *Vice President, NG Book Manufacturing*
George Bounelis, *Vice President, Production Services*
Nicole Elliott, *Manager*
Rachel Faulise, *Manager*
Robert L. Barr, *Manager*

CELEBRATING 125 YEARS

The National Geographic Society is one of the world's largest nonprofit scientific and educational organizations. Founded in 1888 to "increase and diffuse geographic knowledge," the Society's mission is to inspire people to care about the planet. It reaches more than 400 million people worldwide each month through its official journal, *National Geographic*, and other magazines; National Geographic Channel; television documentaries; music; radio; films; books; DVDs; maps; exhibitions; live events; school publishing programs; interactive media; and merchandise. National Geographic has funded more than 10,000 scientific research, conservation and exploration projects and supports an education program promoting geographic literacy.

For more information, please call 1-800-NGS LINE (647-5463) or write to the following address:

National Geographic Society, 1145 17th Street N.W., Washington, D.C. 20036-4688 U.S.A.

Visit us online at www.nationalgeographic.com/books

For librarians and teachers: www.ngchildrensbooks.org

More for kids from National Geographic: kids.nationalgeographic.com

For information about special discounts for bulk purchases, please contact National Geographic Books Special Sales: ngspecsales@ngs.org

For rights or permissions inquiries, please contact National Geographic Books Subsidiary Rights: ngbookrights@ngs.org

Library of Congress Control Number: 2013933647

ISBN: 978-1-4263-1355-4

Printed in Hong Kong

13/THK/1